Grandpa...Why Are You Planting That Tree?

Grandpa...Why Are You Planting That Tree?

Ted Hoagland

by
Ted Hoagland

AuthorHouse™
1663 Liberty Drive
Bloomington, IN 47403
www.authorhouse.com
Phone: 833-262-8899

Because of the dynamic nature of the Internet, any web addresses or links contained in this book may have changed since publication and may no longer be valid. The views expressed in this work are solely those of the author and do not necessarily reflect the views of the publisher, and the publisher hereby disclaims any responsibility for them.

This book is printed on acid-free paper.

ISBN: 978-1-4259-7743-6 (sc)

Print information available on the last page.

Published by AuthorHouse 04/14/2022

authorHOUSE®

GRANDPA-

...WHY ARE YOU PLANTING THAT TREE?

Author: Ted Hoagland
Illustrated by Kris Steil

Animals and birds would not have food or a home…they would be left out in the cold and all alone.

Remember...trees are alive ...

they grow - they breathe.

...and what they breathe out

is air that we need.

All plants have feet just like you.

They are called roots and help trees find water.

Feet of trees do not walk or run.

Instead those feet hold trees in place so they will

grow greener and taller.

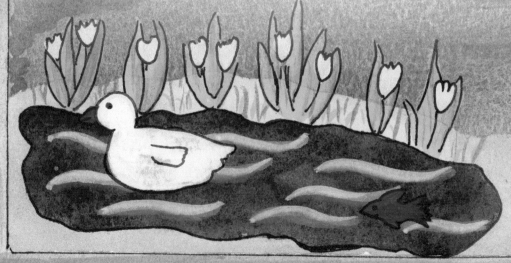

But, when it gets cold and days

get shorter, leaves stop making

chlorophyll and begin to turn brown.

Leaves also turn yellow, red, and

orange before they fall to the ground!

Leaves are important because that is where

trees get their food and...

...they grow big and beautiful just like you.

Trees lose water through their leaves-

so when leaves fall,

trees hold water and

stay well fed.

Other trees don't lose their leaves
and are called Evergreen.

Some have leaves called needles

which are very thin and even in the

winter are always green.

Holly trees also have evergreen leaves

that seem like leather to the touch...

and since Holly leaves are thicker,

they do not lose water as much.

But, why do trees grow so tall

and stand in place?

Olivia, trees don't have bones like you and me but have a substance called lignin.

Lignin and a skin called bark allow trees to grow tall and stand very straight.

So…without trees we would not

have fresh air to breath and leaves

the colors of a rainbow-

…and some of our animal friends

would not have a home or

the food they need to grow.

The author is a grandpa to Olivia, Nick, Zach, Jacob, and Genevieve, and an instructor of Botany and Plant

Morphology at Christopher Newport University in Newport News, Virginia.

Printed in the United States
by Baker & Taylor Publisher Services